World of Reptiles

Crocodiles

by Adele Richardson

Consultants:
The Staff of Reptile Gardens
Rapid City, South Dakota

Mankato, Minnesota

Bridgestone Books are published by Capstone Press,
151 Good Counsel Drive, P.O. Box 669, Mankato, Minnesota 56002.
www.capstonepress.com

Library of Congress Cataloging-in-Publication Data
Richardson, Adele, 1966–
    Crocodiles / by Adele Richardson.
       p. cm.—(Bridgestone Books. World of reptiles)
    Includes bibliographical references and index.
    ISBN 0-7368-4327-2 (hardcover)
    1. Crocodiles—Juvenile literature. I. Title. II. Series.
QL666.C925R522 2006
597.98'2—dc22   2004027943

Summary: A brief introduction to crocodiles, discussing their characteristics, range, habitat, food, offspring, and dangers. Includes a range map, life cycle diagram, and amazing facts.

Editorial Credits
Shari Joffe, editor; Enoch Peterson, set designer; Biner Design, book designer; Patricia Rasch, illustrator; Jo Miller, photo researcher; Scott Thoms, photo editor

Photo Credits
Bruce Coleman Inc./Robert E. Pelham, cover
Corbis/Gavriel Jecan, 20
Creatas, 1
James P. Rowan, 6
Nature Picture Library/Anup Shah, 12, 18
Pete Carmichael, 4
Peter Arnold, Inc./Sunset, 16
Tom & Pat Leeson, 10

Table of Contents

4

Crocodiles

Crocodiles are named for how they look. "Crocodile" comes from a Greek word that means "pebble worm." The skin of these long reptiles looks hard and rocky.

As reptiles, crocodiles have scales, are **cold-blooded**, and come from eggs. They are closely related to alligators, but they have some differences. Crocodiles have long, V-shaped noses. Alligators' noses are shorter and wider. Crocodiles have teeth that stick out when their mouths are closed. When an alligator closes its mouth, no lower teeth show.

◄ The scales on a crocodile's back are hard and thick, like armor.

What Crocodiles Look Like

Crocodiles have long bodies and tails. Their four legs are short and strong. Their webbed toes have claws.

A crocodile's skin is covered with thick scales. Most crocodiles are brown, gray, or greenish. Some have dark markings. Crocodiles also have bony plates under the skin on their backs.

Crocodiles have about 68 sharp teeth. If a tooth wears out, a new tooth grows in its place. Crocodiles grow thousands of teeth during their lives.

◄ Crocodiles have sharp teeth and powerful jaws.

Crocodile Range Map

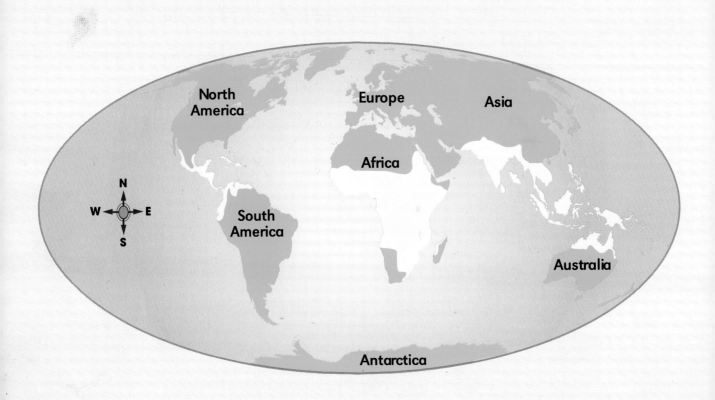

North
America

Europe

Asia

Africa

N
W ◆ E
S

South
America

Australia

Antarctica

☐ Where Crocodiles Live

Crocodiles in the World

Crocodiles live in warm waters in many parts of the world. There are fourteen kinds of crocodiles. Most live in Africa, Australia, India, and Southeast Asia. Several kinds of crocodiles are found in Central and South America. The American crocodile lives in coastal areas from the southern tip of Florida to Venezuela.

Crocodile Habitats

Crocodiles live in wetland **habitats**. Most are found in freshwater swamps, rivers, and **marshes**. Some crocodiles live in streams.

Several kinds of crocodiles spend their time in **brackish** water. Brackish water is a mixture of fresh water and salty water. The slender-snouted crocodile of Africa and the American crocodile often live in brackish water. The Australian saltwater crocodile can sometimes be seen swimming far out to sea.

◄ This American crocodile lives near a river.

What Crocodiles Eat

Crocodiles hunt other animals for food. They eat fish, turtles, birds, and mammals. Nile crocodiles often eat large animals such as wildebeests, zebras, and impalas.

A crocodile usually hunts at night. It floats silently in water and waits for **prey** to come near. Then it leaps out of the water and grabs the prey with its strong jaws.

Crocodiles do not chew their food. They tear off chunks to swallow. Small animals are swallowed whole. Crocodiles sometimes share large prey with other crocodiles.

◄ A Nile crocodile grabs a young wildebeest.

The Life Cycle of a Crocodile

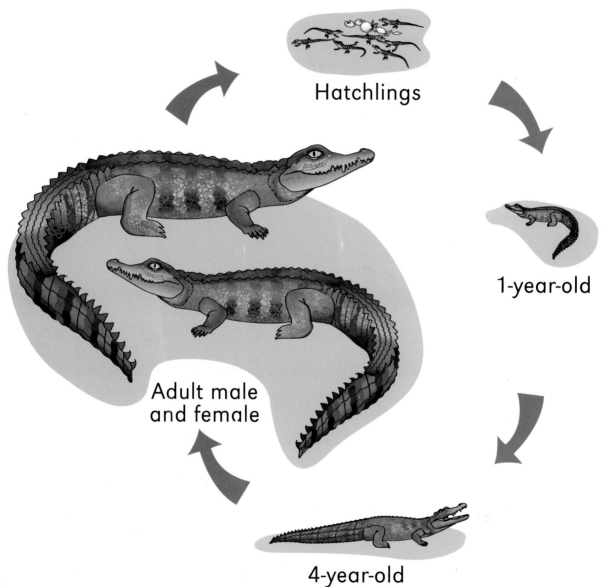

Hatchlings

1-year-old

4-year-old

Adult male
and female

Producing Young

Male and female crocodiles **mate** in the water to produce young. After mating, the female crocodile builds a nest on land. Some crocodiles make a large pile of leaves and mud. Others dig a hole in sand.

The female lays between 15 and 90 eggs in the nest. The eggs hatch in about 90 days. Crocodile mothers often help the young to hatch. They open the nest or gently break open the eggs with their mouths.

Growing Up

Crocodiles are about 10 inches (25 centimeters) long when they hatch. Crocodile mothers scoop up the young in their mouths and take them to water.

Young crocodiles eat insects and small fish. They stay close to their mothers for protection. While in the water, they may ride on their mothers' backs or heads. Crocodile young stay with their mothers for two to three years.

◄ A female crocodile gently holds her young in her mouth.

Dangers to Crocodiles

Young crocodiles have many **predators**. Other reptiles, birds, and some mammals eat young crocodiles or crocodile eggs.

People are the greatest danger to adult crocodiles. People hunt crocodiles for their meat and skins. They also destroy crocodile habitats. Many kinds of crocodiles are **endangered**.

Many countries now have laws to protect crocodiles. In some places, land has been set aside for crocodiles. People are working to make sure these reptiles do not disappear.

◄ A monitor lizard steals a crocodile egg. Very few crocodiles make it from egg to adult.

Amazing Facts about Crocodiles

- A crocodile can sneak up on prey by swimming with only its eyes, ears, and nose showing above the water.
- The saltwater crocodile is the largest living reptile. It can be as long as 23 feet (7 meters).
- Crocodiles really do cry "crocodile tears." But it's not because they're sad. Their eyes water to clean out dirt or dust.
- Crocodiles don't sweat. They cool their bodies by lying still with their mouths open.

◀ When a crocodile floats, only its eyes, ears, and nose show above the water.

Glossary

brackish (BRACK-ish)—made up of a mixture of freshwater and salty water

cold-blooded (KOHLD-BLUHD-id)—having a body temperature that is the same as its surroundings; all reptiles are cold-blooded.

endangered (en-DAYN-jurd)—at risk of dying out

habitat (HAB-uh-tat)—the place and natural conditions where an animal lives

marsh (MARSH)—an area of low land covered with shallow water

mate (MAYT)—to join together to produce young

predator (PRED-uh-tur)—an animal that hunts other animals for food

prey (PRAY)—an animal hunted by another animal for food

Read More

Markle, Sandra. *Crocodiles.* Animal Predators. Minneapolis: Carolrhoda Books, 2004.

Murray, Julie. *Crocodiles.* Animal Kingdom. Edina, Minn.: Abdo Publishing, 2005.

Internet Sites

FactHound offers a safe, fun way to find Internet sites related to this book. All of the sites on FactHound have been researched by our staff.

Here's how:
1. Visit *www.facthound.com*
2. Type in this special code **0736843272** for age-appropriate sites. Or enter a search word related to this book for a more general search.
3. Click on the **Fetch It** button.

FactHound will fetch the best sites for you!

Index